Little Pebble™

Farm Facts

Machines on the Farm

by Lisa J. Amstutz

PEBBLE
a capstone imprint

For my farming family. Miss you, Dad, and proud of you, Tyler. –Ashlee

Pebble Books are published by Pebble
1710 Roe Crest Drive
North Mankato, Minnesota 56003
www.mycapstone.com

Library of Congress Cataloging-in-Publication Data
is available on the Library of Congress website.
ISBN 978-1-9771-0257-7 (library binding)
ISBN 978-1-9771-0537-0 (paperback)
ISBN 978-1-9771-0262-1 (eBook PDF)
Summary: Invites beginning readers to ride along
on a number of common farm vehicles, including
tractors, planters, and combines, and explains
the machines' roles, particularly as they pertain to
crop farming.

Editorial Credits

Jill Kalz, editor; Ashlee Suker, designer;
Kelly Garvin, media researcher;
Katy LaVigne, production specialist

Photo Credits

Ashlee Suker 21; iStockphoto/Slavica, 17;
Shutterstock: Brian A Jackson, 2, Fotokostic, 11,
13, mihalec, 15, Ollyy, 5, oticki, 10, Peter Gudella,
3, 20, photosOK, 14, Rihardzz, 19, schubbel, 18,
Sergey Belyshev, backcover, 7, smereka, cover,
Somchai Sanvongchaiya, 9, suwatsilp sooksang, 8
(top), VRstudio, 1, 8 (bottom)

Design Element

Shutterstock: Dudarev Mikhail, J.Schelkle,
K.Narloch-Liberra, laura.h, Sichon

Printed and bound in China.
966

Table of Contents

Working Together

Farmers do many jobs on a farm. They work hard. Machines help them. Let's watch!

Time to Grow

Some tractors lift. Others pull.
They all move heavy loads.

Plows dig up the soil.
They get it ready
for planting.

A planter sows seeds.

See the rows? Neat!

The seeds grow. So do weeds.
They hurt crops. Farmers try
to get rid of weeds.

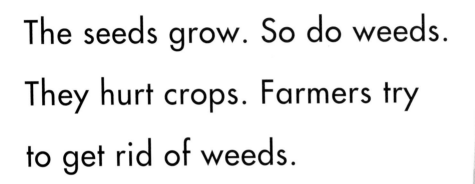

Cut and Store

Look! The wheat is tall.

It is ready for cutting.

Chop! Chop!

The grain goes
into a truck.

The straw falls away.

A baler picks up the straw.

It makes bales.

Many farm animals sleep on straw.

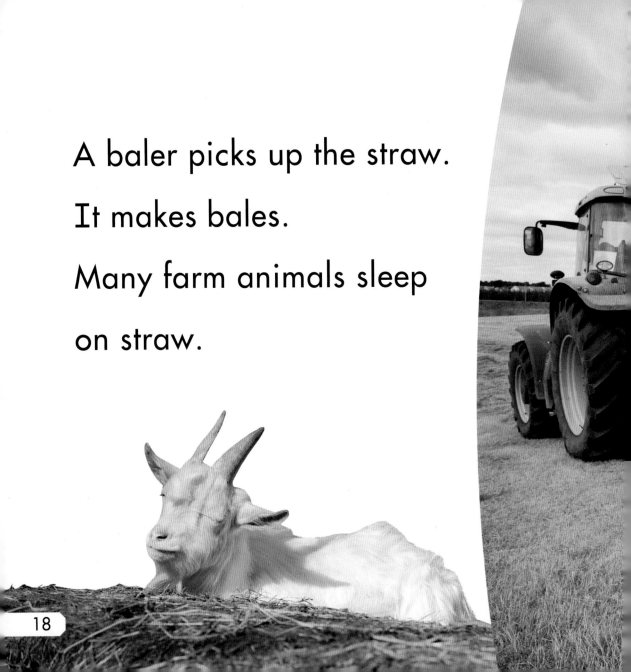

Thank you, machines!

You make work easier!

Glossary

bale—a large bundle of straw or hay tied tightly together; a baler is a machine that makes bales

crop—a plant farmers grow in large amounts, usually for food

grain—the seed of a grassy plant such as wheat, rice, corn, rye, or barley

machine—a piece of equipment that is used to do a job

plow—a machine that turns over soil

soil—another word for dirt

sow—to plant

straw—the dried stems of wheat, barley, or oat plants

weed—a plant that grows where it is not wanted

Read More

Borth, Teddy. *Machines on the Farm.* On the Farm. Minneapolis: Abdo Kids, 2015.

Clay, Kathryn. *Farm Machines.* Wild About Wheels. North Mankato, Minn.: Capstone Press, a Capstone imprint, 2015.

West, David. *Farm Machinery.* Mechanic Mike's Machines. Mankato, Minn.: A+, Smart Apple Media, 2015.

Internet Sites

Use FactHound to find Internet sites related to this book.

Visit *www.facthound.com*

Just type in 9781977102577 and go.

Check out projects, games and lots more at
www.capstonekids.com

Critical Thinking Questions

1. How do tractors help farmers?

2. What do plows do?

3. Why do farmers try to get rid of weeds?

Index